15 Classical Master
with Added Second Piano Parts

Intermediate to Early Advanced
(Two Pianos, Four Hands)
Second Piano Parts by Sylvia Rabinof

Alfred's Classic Editions

Copyright © MMVIII by Alfred Publishing Co., Inc.
All Rights Reserved. Printed in USA.
ISBN-10: 0-7390-5720-0
ISBN-13: 978-0-7390-5720-9

Table of Contents

MUSETTE (from *Notebook for Anna Magdalena*)
Johann Sebastian Bach (1685–1750). 4

MINUET IN G MAJOR (from *Notebook for Anna Magdalena*)
Johann Sebastian Bach (1685–1750). 8

MINUET IN G MINOR (from *Notebook for Anna Magdalena*)
Johann Sebastian Bach (1685–1750). 10

FÜR ELISE
Ludwig van Beethoven (1770–1827). 13

CHACONNE ON AIR "DIDO'S LAMENT" (from the opera *Dido and Aeneas*)
Henry Purcell (1659–1695) 26

LÄNDLER IN D MAJOR
Ludwig van Beethoven (1770–1827). 34

LÄNDLER IN A MINOR
Franz Schubert (1797–1828) 36

THE HAPPY FARMER
Robert Schumann (1810–1856) 39

POUR LE LUTE (Little Prelude No. 3 in C Minor)
Johann Sebastian Bach (1685–1750) 42

INVENTION NO. 8 IN F MAJOR
Johann Sebastian Bach (1685–1750) 47

SOLFEGGIETTO
Carl Philipp Emanuel Bach (1714–1788) 51

RONDO ALLA TURCA (from *Sonata in A Major*, K. 331)
Wolfgang Amadeus Mozart (1756–1791) 57

INVENTION NO. 13 IN A MINOR
Johann Sebastian Bach (1685–1750) 65

CLAIR DE LUNE (from *Suite bergamasque*)
Claude Debussy (1862–1918) 69

SONATA IN C MAJOR, K. 545 (First Movement)
Wolfgang Amadeus Mozart (1756–1791) 79

Foreword

"I believe that anyone can improvise."
—Sylvia Rabinof (1913–2001)

Born in New York City on October 10, 1913, Sylvia Rabinof (neé Smith) showed at a young age an enthusiasm and flair for both performing and improvising at the piano. The legendary Ignacy Paderewski and Rudolf Serkin were among her early teachers, and she made her Town Hall debut at the age of 25. A few years later she met violinist Benno Rabinof, who would become her husband and with whom she embarked on a concertizing career that lasted until his death in 1975. The couple toured the world playing works for violin and piano, while also keeping a busy teaching schedule. Sylvia taught in the pre-college division at The Juilliard School, and was on the faculty at SUNY Fredonia.

Sylvia was also a composer, creating second piano parts for the masterpieces included in this collection. The idea to publish these works began after she accompanied the student of a friend with a second piano part she had written for J. S. Bach's *Minuet in G*. Both the student and her teacher were thrilled by the composition and urged her to write more. This developed into an entire series of works based on her original improvisations. The publishing of these pieces provided the musical world with beautiful accompaniments for many classic pieces, as well as insight into the mind of one of the world's great improvisers. Rabinof hoped to encourage modern pianists to try their own hands at improvisation, just as the great composers and pianists of the 18th- and 19th-centuries had. She often pointed out that Bach, Beethoven, Liszt and others were all masters of this art and that, with practice, any pianist could become one as well.

Musette

from *Notebook for Anna Magdalena*

Johann Sebastian Bach
Second piano part by Sylvia Rabinof

Minuet in G Major
from *Notebook for Anna Magdalena*

Johann Sebastian Bach
Second piano part by Sylvia Rabinof

Minuet in G Minor

from *Notebook for Anna Magdalena*

Johann Sebastian Bach
Second piano part by Sylvia Rabinof

Für Elise

Ludwig van Beethoven
Second piano part by Sylvia Rabinof

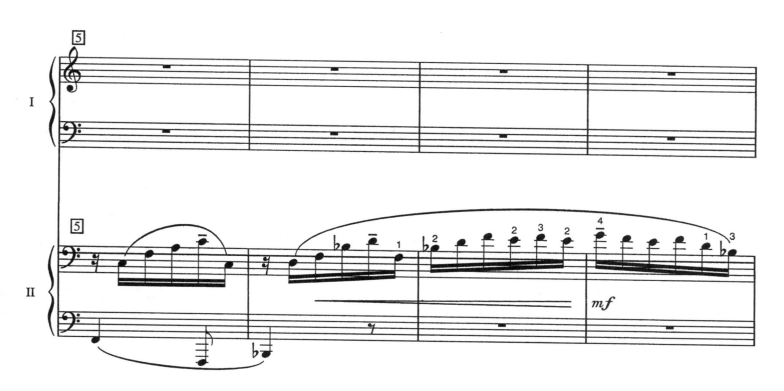

to Charles

Chaconne on Air "Dido's Lament"

from the opera *Dido and Aeneas*

Henry Purcell
Second piano part by Sylvia Rabinof

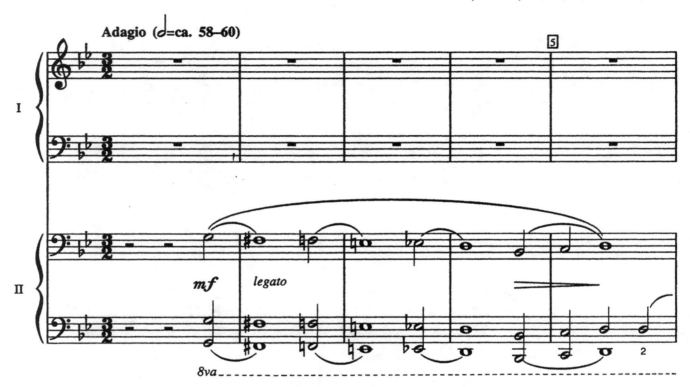

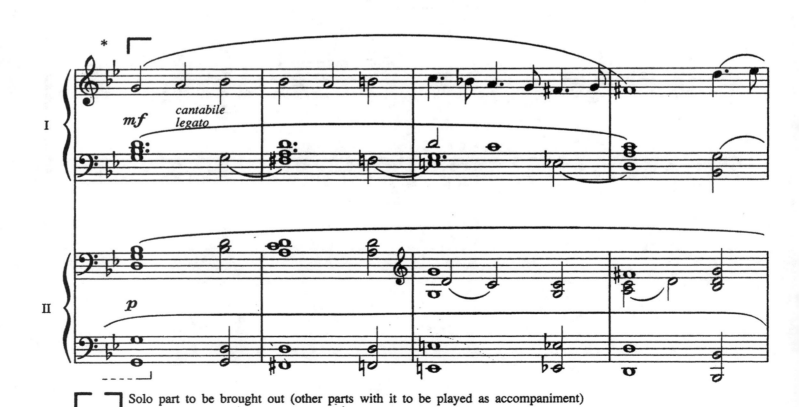

⌐ ¬ Solo part to be brought out (other parts with it to be played as accompaniment)

Ländler in D Major

Ludwig van Beethoven
Second piano part by Sylvia Rabinof

* easier: ⊛ easier:

Ländler in A Minor

Franz Schubert
Second piano part by Sylvia Rabinof

* Piano Two should be about one level softer than Piano One throughout.

The Happy Farmer

Robert Schumann
Second piano part by Sylvia Rabinof

Pour le Lute

Little Prelude No. 3 in C Minor

Johann Sebastian Bach
Second piano part by Sylvia Rabinof

Invention No. 8 in F Major

Johann Sebastian Bach
Second piano part by Sylvia Rabinof

Solfeggietto

Carl Phillipp Emanuel Bach
Second piano part by Sylvia Rabinof

Rondo Alla Turca

from *Sonata in A Major*, K. 331

Wolfgang Amadeus Mozart
Second piano part by Sylvia Rabinof

Invention No. 13 in A Minor

Johann Sebastian Bach
Second piano part by Sylvia Rabinof

Clair de Lune

from *Suite bergamasque*

Claude Debussy
Second piano part by Sylvia Rabinof

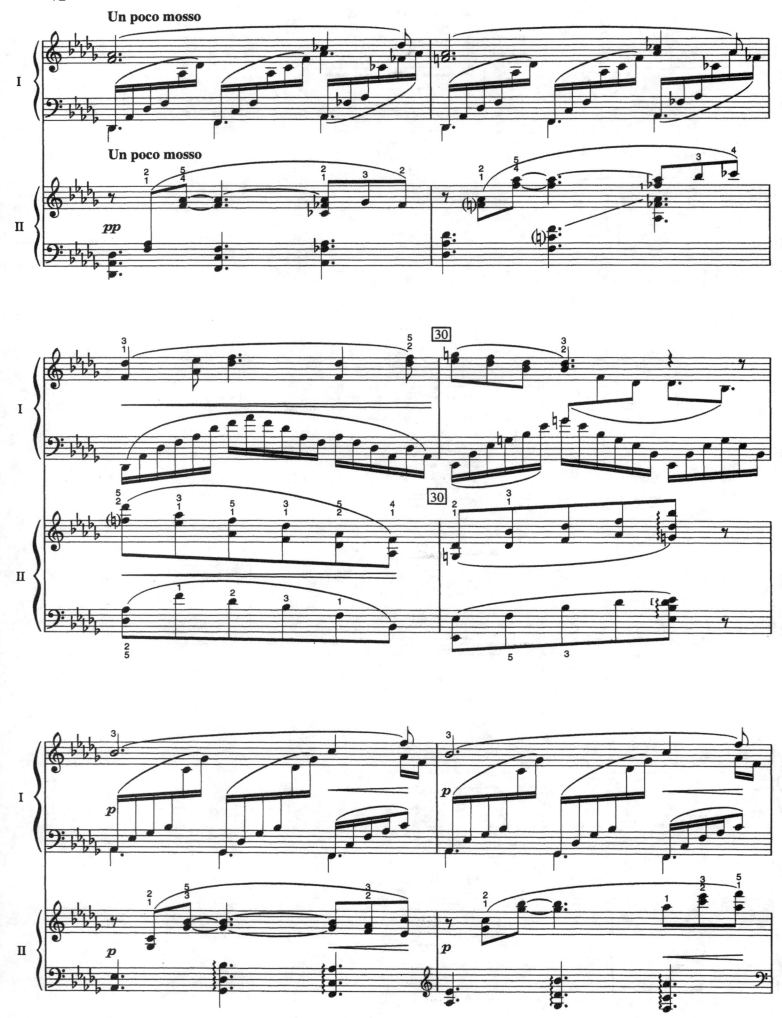

Sonata in C Major, K. 545
(First Movement)

Wolfgang Amadeus Mozart
Second piano part by Sylvia Rabinof